D0484323

PAPER AIRPLANES!

A SHOW-HOW GUIDE!

Written & illustrated
by Keith Zoo

ODD DOT • NEW YORK

Hey there!

This **Show-How** gives you the know-how on paper airplanes. We've included only the essentials so you can easily master the FUN-damentals. You'll be flying in no time. Ready? Let's go!

MATERIALS NEEDED:

PAPER
(US letter size works best for these planes)

RULER

SCISSORS

PAPER CLIPS

EACH PAPER AIRPLANE IN THIS BOOK INCLUDES THE FOLLOWING STATS:

Speed: How fast it goes

Airtime: How long it stays in the air

Distance: How far it goes, from where it takes off to where it lands

Acrobatics: If the plane spins, swirls, or swoops

Uniqueness: How different it looks, beyond the basic design

TABLE OF CONTENTS

TIPS FOR SOARING SUCCESS!

Folds: Before pressing down, make sure everything lines up. Take your time to make crisp folds. Any folds that are out of alignment or crooked will cause your plane to fly poorly.

Symmetry: Whatever you do on one side, make sure it matches the other, or the plane won't fly straight.

Handling: Once you've made your plane, handle it carefully! Any crumples to the nose or wings will throw off its ability to fly.

Flying: You should always start with a test flight, one that's nice and light. You'll see how your plane flies and if you need to make any adjustments. You may need to go back and refold in places. If it all checks out, let it soar!

Start over: Some of these planes are pretty tricky. If you need to start over, go for it! See if you can reuse the retired plane as doodle paper for a fun drawing, take notes on it, or recycle it.

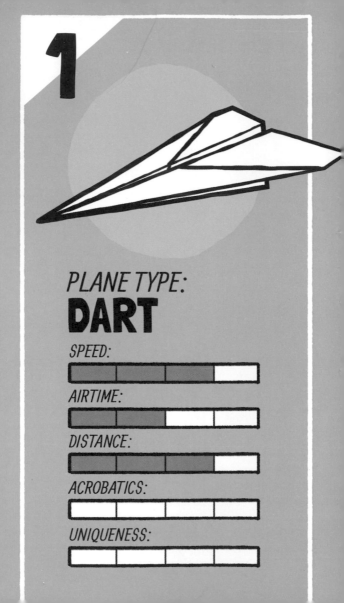

1

PLANE TYPE:
DART

SPEED:

AIRTIME:

DISTANCE:

ACROBATICS:

UNIQUENESS:

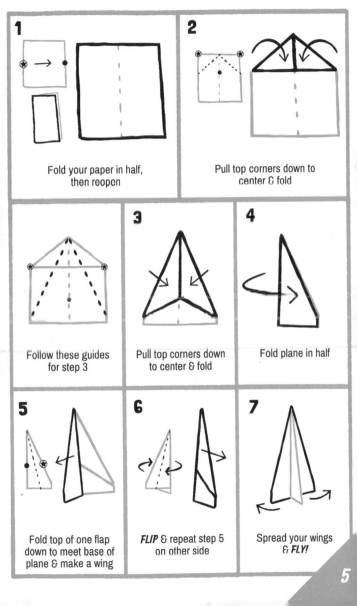

1

Fold your paper in half, then reopen

2

Pull top corners down to center & fold

3

Follow these guides for step 3

Pull top corners down to center & fold

4

Fold plane in half

5

Fold top of one flap down to meet base of plane & make a wing

6

FLIP & repeat step 5 on other side

7

Spread your wings & *FLY!*

2

PLANE TYPE:
BULLDOG DART

SPEED:

AIRTIME:

DISTANCE:

ACROBATICS:

UNIQUENESS:

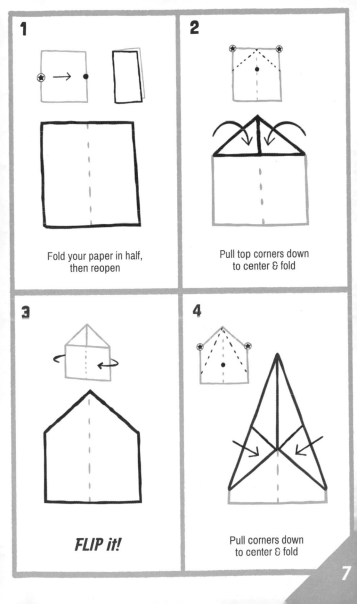

1

Fold your paper in half, then reopen

2

Pull top corners down to center & fold

3

FLIP it!

4

Pull corners down to center & fold

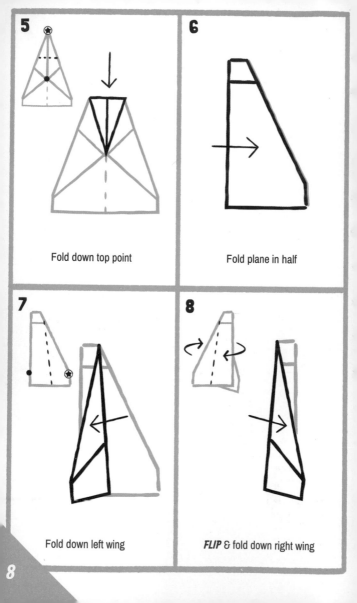

5

Fold down top point

6

Fold plane in half

7

Fold down left wing

8

FLIP & fold down right wing

9

Spread your wings & *FLY!*

3

PLANE TYPE:
EAGLE

SPEED:

AIRTIME:

DISTANCE:

ACROBATICS:

UNIQUENESS:

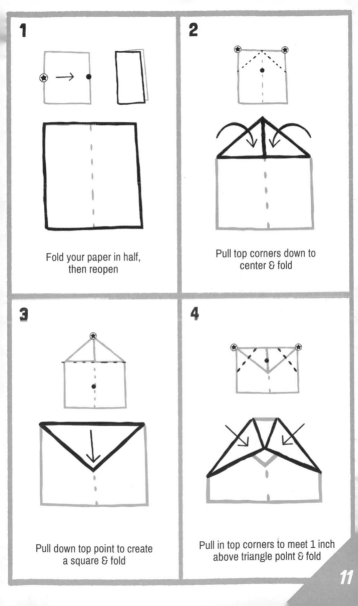

1

Fold your paper in half, then reopen

2

Pull top corners down to center & fold

3

Pull down top point to create a square & fold

4

Pull in top corners to meet 1 inch above triangle point & fold

11

5

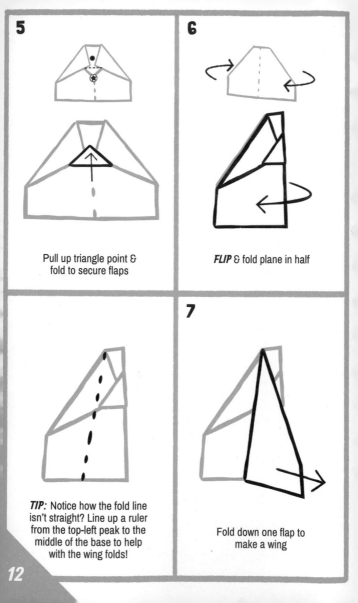

Pull up triangle point &
fold to secure flaps

6

FLIP & fold plane in half

TIP: Notice how the fold line
isn't straight? Line up a ruler
from the top-left peak to the
middle of the base to help
with the wing folds!

7

Fold down one flap to
make a wing

8

FLIP & repeat step 7 on the other side

9

Spread your wings & **_FLY!_**

It's okay to get frustrated . . .

DON'T GIVE UP!

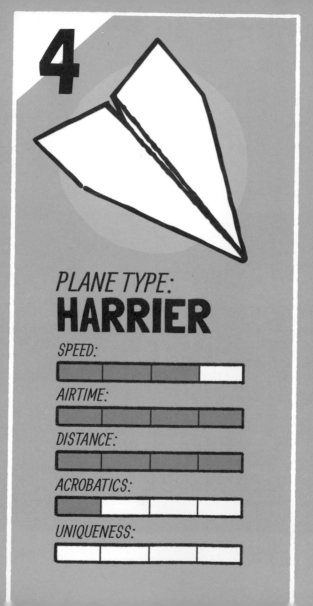

4

PLANE TYPE:
HARRIER

SPEED:

AIRTIME:

DISTANCE:

ACROBATICS:

UNIQUENESS:

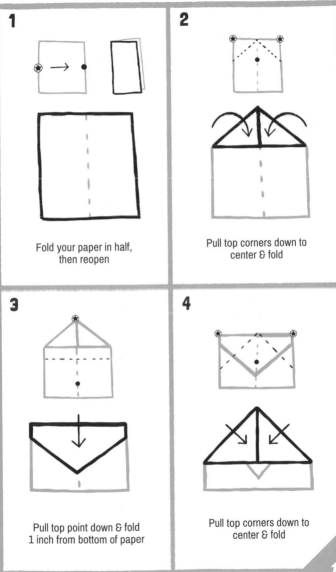

1

Fold your paper in half, then reopen

2

Pull top corners down to center & fold

3

Pull top point down & fold 1 inch from bottom of paper

4

Pull top corners down to center & fold

15

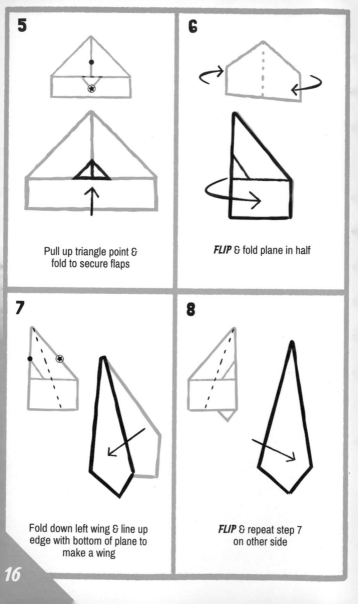

5

Pull up triangle point &
fold to secure flaps

6

FLIP & fold plane in half

7

Fold down left wing & line up
edge with bottom of plane to
make a wing

8

FLIP & repeat step 7
on other side

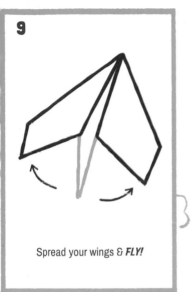

9

Spread your wings & *FLY!*

5

PLANE TYPE:
V-WING

SPEED:

AIRTIME:

DISTANCE:

ACROBATICS:

UNIQUENESS:

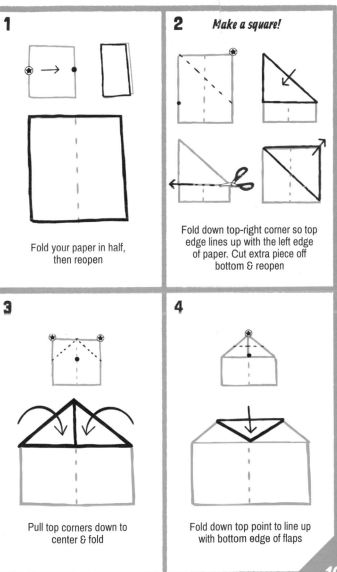

1

Fold your paper in half, then reopen

2 *Make a square!*

Fold down top-right corner so top edge lines up with the left edge of paper. Cut extra piece off bottom & reopen

3

Pull top corners down to center & fold

4

Fold down top point to line up with bottom edge of flaps

19

5

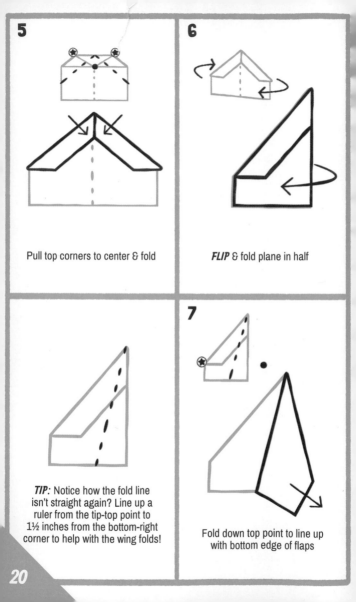

Pull top corners to center & fold

6

FLIP & fold plane in half

TIP: Notice how the fold line isn't straight again? Line up a ruler from the tip-top point to 1½ inches from the bottom-right corner to help with the wing folds!

7

Fold down top point to line up with bottom edge of flaps

20

8

FLIP & repeat step 7 on other side

9

Spread your wings & **FLY!**

TIP!

Use your discarded paper from step 2 to make two helicopter planes (see page 42 for instructions!).

21

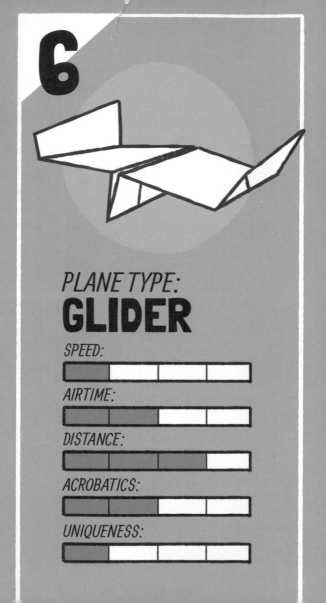

6

PLANE TYPE:
GLIDER

SPEED:

AIRTIME:

DISTANCE:

ACROBATICS:

UNIQUENESS:

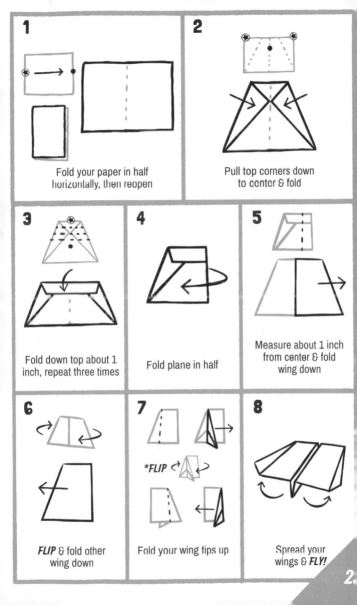

1

Fold your paper in half horizontally, then reopen

2

Pull top corners down to center & fold

3

Fold down top about 1 inch, repeat three times

4

Fold plane in half

5

Measure about 1 inch from center & fold wing down

6

FLIP & fold other wing down

7

FLIP

Fold your wing tips up

8

Spread your wings & **FLY!**

27

7

PLANE TYPE:
BOOMERANG

SPEED:

AIRTIME:

DISTANCE:

ACROBATICS:

UNIQUENESS:

1

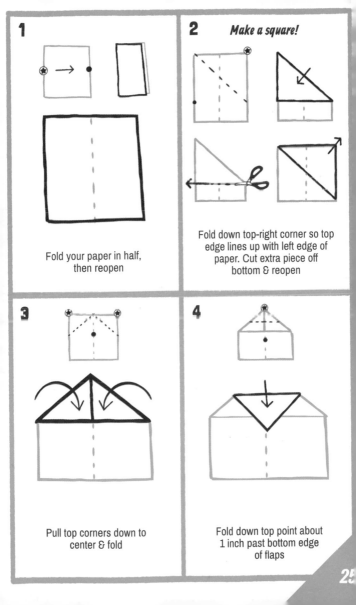

Fold your paper in half, then reopen

2
Make a square!

Fold down top-right corner so top edge lines up with left edge of paper. Cut extra piece off bottom & reopen

3

Pull top corners down to center & fold

4

Fold down top point about 1 inch past bottom edge of flaps

25

5

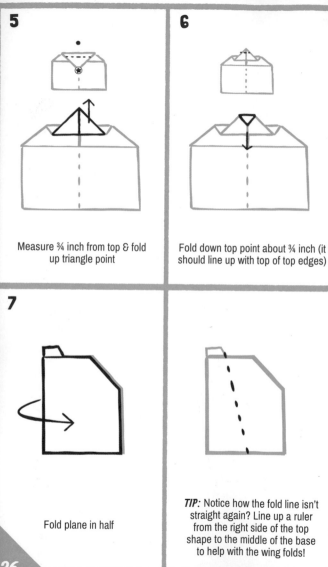

Measure ¾ inch from top & fold up triangle point

6

Fold down top point about ¾ inch (it should line up with top of top edges)

7

Fold plane in half

TIP: Notice how the fold line isn't straight again? Line up a ruler from the right side of the top shape to the middle of the base to help with the wing folds!

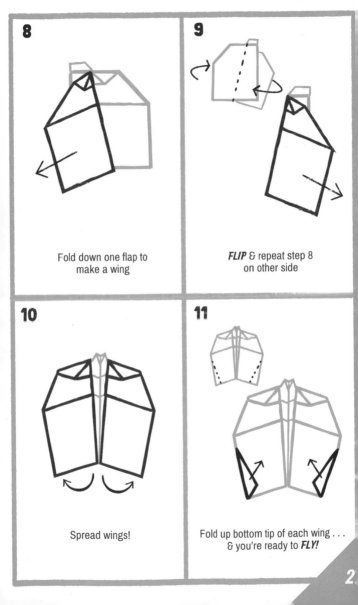

8

Fold down one flap to make a wing

9

FLIP & repeat step 8 on other side

10

Spread wings!

11

Fold up bottom tip of each wing . . . & you're ready to *FLY!*

2

8

PLANE TYPE:
HAMMER

SPEED:

AIRTIME:

DISTANCE:

ACROBATICS:

UNIQUENESS:

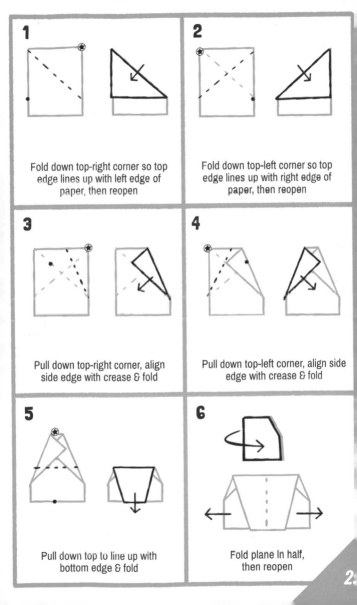

1

Fold down top-right corner so top edge lines up with left edge of paper, then reopen

2

Fold down top-left corner so top edge lines up with right edge of paper, then reopen

3

Pull down top-right corner, align side edge with crease & fold

4

Pull down top-left corner, align side edge with crease & fold

5

Pull down top to line up with bottom edge & fold

6

Fold plane in half, then reopen

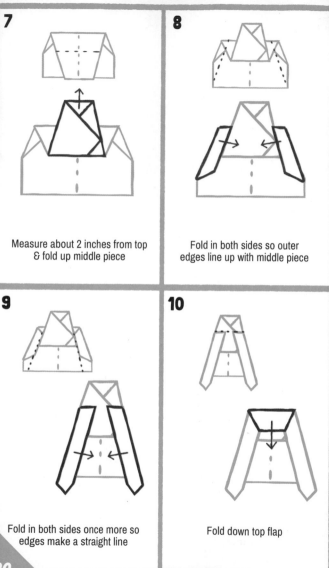

7

Measure about 2 inches from top & fold up middle piece

8

Fold in both sides so outer edges line up with middle piece

9

Fold in both sides once more so edges make a straight line

10

Fold down top flap

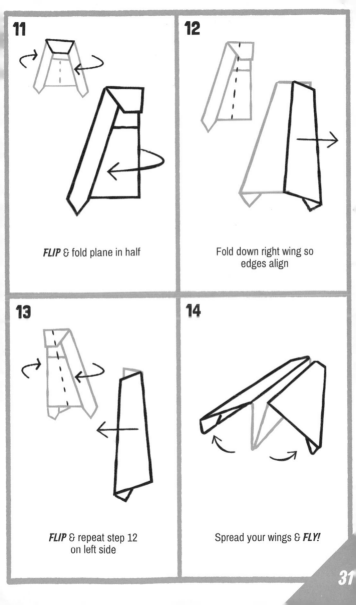

11

FLIP & fold plane in half

12

Fold down right wing so
edges align

13

FLIP & repeat step 12
on left side

14

Spread your wings & *FLY!*

9

PLANE TYPE:
CROSSWING

SPEED:

AIRTIME:

DISTANCE:

ACROBATICS:

UNIQUENESS:

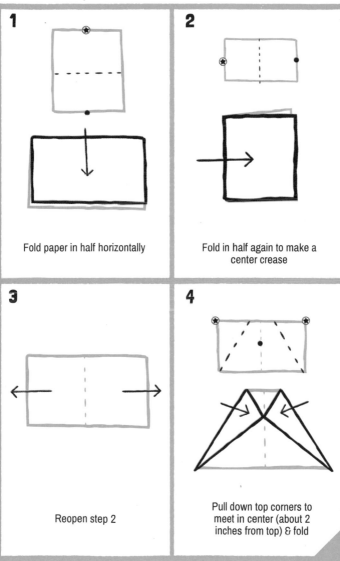

1

Fold paper in half horizontally

2

Fold in half again to make a center crease

3

Reopen step 2

4

Pull down top corners to meet in center (about 2 inches from top) & fold

5

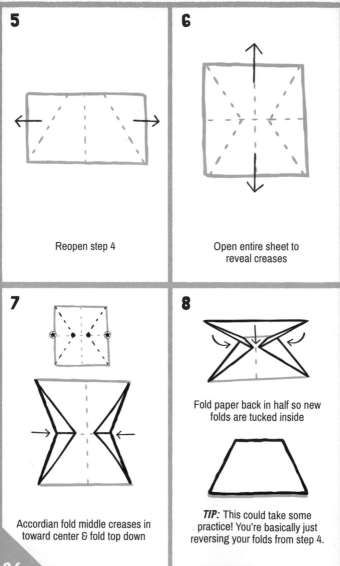

Reopen step 4

6

Open entire sheet to
reveal creases

7

Accordian fold middle creases in
toward center & fold top down

8

Fold paper back in half so new
folds are tucked inside

TIP: This could take some
practice! You're basically just
reversing your folds from step 4.

34

TIP: If you hold your paper up to the light, it should look like this:

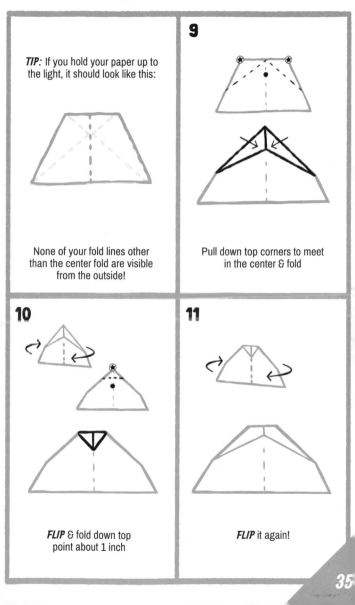

None of your fold lines other than the center fold are visible from the outside!

9

Pull down top corners to meet in the center & fold

10

FLIP & fold down top point about 1 inch

11

FLIP it again!

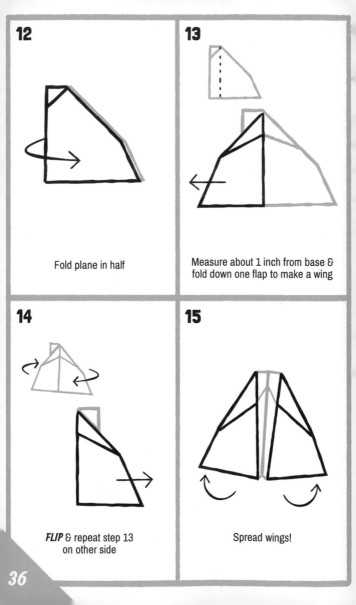

12

Fold plane in half

13

Measure about 1 inch from base &
fold down one flap to make a wing

14

FLIP & repeat step 13
on other side

15

Spread wings!

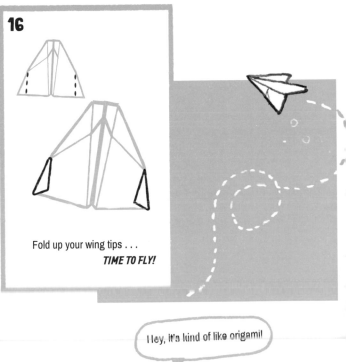

Fold up your wing tips . . .
TIME TO FLY!

Hey, it's kind of like origami!

10

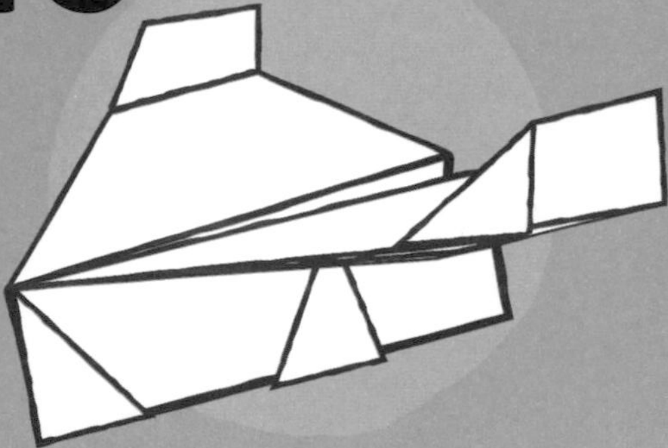

PLANE TYPE:
TRICKSTER

SPEED:

AIRTIME:

DISTANCE:

ACROBATICS:

UNIQUENESS:

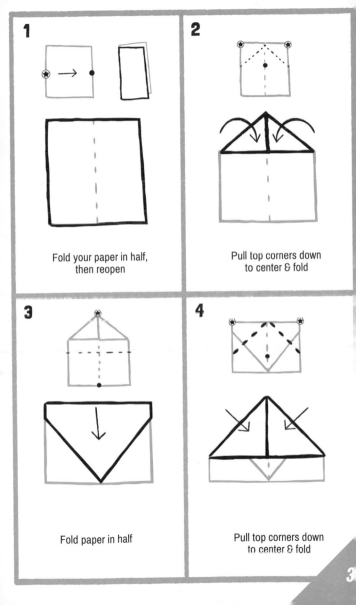

1

Fold your paper in half, then reopen

2

Pull top corners down to center & fold

3

Fold paper in half

4

Pull top corners down to center & fold

3

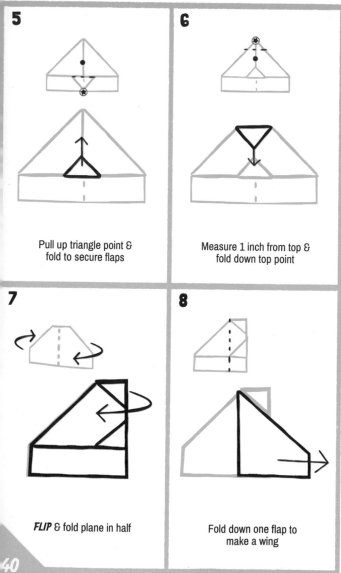

5

Pull up triangle point &
fold to secure flaps

6

Measure 1 inch from top &
fold down top point

7

FLIP & fold plane in half

8

Fold down one flap to
make a wing

9

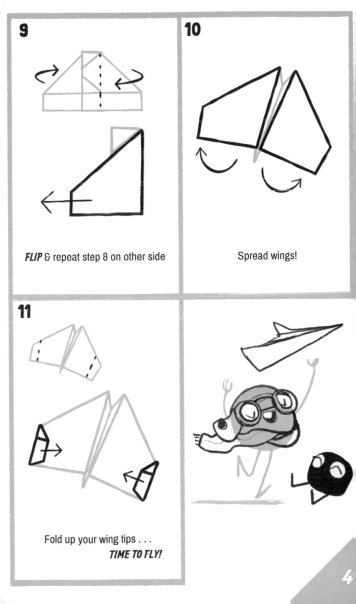

FLIP & repeat step 8 on other side

10

Spread wings!

11

Fold up your wing tips . . .
TIME TO FLY!

4

11

PLANE TYPE:
HELICOPTER

SPEED:

AIRTIME:

DISTANCE:

ACROBATICS:

UNIQUENESS:

1

Cut your paper in half

2

Discard one piece, position other piece horizontally & cut in half

3

Discard one piece, position other piece so it's tallest vertically & cut in half

4

Discard one piece. The last piece should be about 2 inches wide & 5½ inches tall

TIP: Do this with seven other friends & you'll use an entire sheet of paper!

5

Grab a pencil!
Draw these lines on your paper.

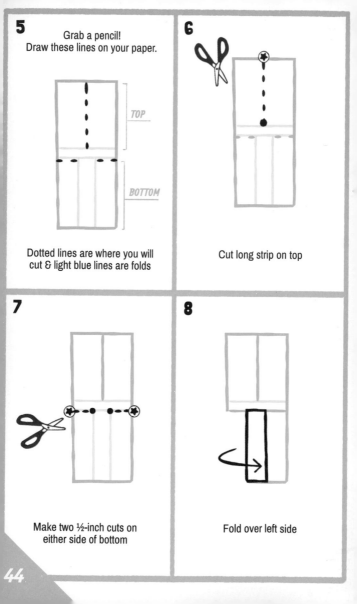

TOP

BOTTOM

Dotted lines are where you will cut & light blue lines are folds

6

Cut long strip on top

7

Make two ½-inch cuts on either side of bottom

8

Fold over left side

9

Fold over right side

10

Fold up bottom ½ inch & secure with a paper clip

11

Fold top strips in opposite directions to make a T shape. These are your wings!

Hold up your helicopter really high and *LET GO!*

TIPS

USE DIFFERENT TYPES OF PAPER!

If you find that you're having trouble keeping your lines straight while you fold your plane, try using **graph paper**.

Does it seem like your plane is super floppy? Maybe it isn't getting the distance you want? Swap your paper out for some nice **construction paper**.

If you want to get really fancy, head over to your local paper supply company and grab some **premium card stock**. These heavier papers will make the biggest impact if you want to fly outside.

EXPERIMENT!

The best part of making a paper airplane is flying it, then making small adjustments. A lot of things can change how your plane flies.

Where you hold the plane with your hand as you launch it into the air will often give you different flight patterns.

How fast you throw the plane will also give you different results. If your plane has a large wingspan, try being a bit more gentle. If you've created a more compact plane built for speed, give it a quick upward throw! Try out different methods. Have fun!

Want to make your plane soar in a particular direction? The tail tips can be bent up or down to make it move different ways. This is helpful if you find that it tends to lean to the right or left, takes a nosedive, or stalls too much. This breakdown should be useful:

LEANS TO THE RIGHT: ***FOLD THE LEFT TAIL DOWNWARD***
LEANS TO THE LEFT: ***FOLD THE RIGHT TAIL DOWNWARD***
NOSE-DIVES: ***BEND THE BACK UPWARD***
STALLS OUT: ***BEND THE BACK DOWNWARD***

Here are a few things we can add to get your newly made flying machine a bit more souped-up.

PAPER CLIPS: Attach this to the front of your plane for an added boost to your distance and speed.

STAPLES: Staple the nose or fuselage (bottom of the plane) to make it sturdier, and for some added speed.

PAPER CLIP & STAPLE COMBO: Staple the front of the plane and add paper clips to the back to increase distance, speed, and sturdiness

TAPE: Tape the seams together for a sturdier construction.

COINS: Toss one or two coins into the fold of your plane to increase the distance covered.

An imprint of Macmillan Publishing Group, LLC
120 Broadway, New York, NY 10271
OddDot.com

Text and illustrations copyright © 2020 by Keith Zoo

Library of Congress Cataloging-in-Publication Data is available.
ISBN 978-1-250-24994-4

Editor: Justin Krasner
Cover designer: Colleen AF Venable & Tim Hall
Interior designer: Colleen AF Venable

Our books may be purchased in bulk for promotional,
educational, or business use. Please contact your local bookseller
or the Macmillan Corporate and Premium Sales Department at
(800) 221-7945 ext. 5442 or by email at
MacmillanSpecialMarkets@macmillan.com.

Show-How Guides is a trademark of Odd Dot.
Printed in China by Hung Hing Off-set Printing Co. Ltd., Heshan City,
Guangdong Province
First edition, 2020

10 9 8 7 6 5 4 3 2 1

Keith Zoo

is an artist and illustrator
living in Massachusetts. You
can find more of his work
at keithzoo.com and on
Instagram @keithzoo.